Just Bee You

A guide to surviving the best bits of life,
and holding your middle finger up to the rest

By
Bindy Hall

Published by and available from
theendlessbookcase.com

Printed Edition
Also available in multiple e-book formats.

The Endless Bookcase Ltd
71 Castle Road, St Albans, Hertfordshire, England,
UK, AL1 5DQ

Book Cover Illustrator
Vivien Blunden: vivienblunden@hotmail.com

Book Editor
Morgana Evans: info@theendlessbookcase.com

ISBN: 978-1-912243-87-7

Dedication.

To the three best people I ever met…
Nathan, Bessie and Bailey xxxx

About The Author.

Bindy Hall B.Sc is a graduate in the fields of psychology and counselling. An avid writer since a very young age- she began her writing career in crayon. Making and handing out homemade books bound in sticky tape to whoever was in her vicinity.

A prolific and repeat swearer, she describes herself as a mixture of sarcasm, hair and empathy, in equal measure. She is a mother of two and wife of one, and is happiest at home and writing.

She wrote 'Just Bee You' in response to the eclectic mix of worries of people around her.

"My thing in life, is to try to help others see their worth. If I can encourage positivity, vanquish a worry or two and improve confidence for just one reader, then sitting up all night writing, heavily caffeinated, cross-legged on my landing- will have been worth it."

Reviews.

"Bindy has a knack of taking my breath away with her work. It's like she knows exactly what makes us tick! My favourite piece is *B is for beautiful* and one particular sentence has stuck with me: *You have an invisible layer of protection, you know this because you make it, every night, when you sleep.* Powerful words, powerful mind, beautiful person."

- Clare Johns, Furniture Finisher.

"Bindy Hall writes pieces that are not only honest, they are relatable. When you read them you smile along, cry at parts, and share the experiences that she is voicing or been of witness too. They enable you to sit back and reflect, think and realise you are not alone and that is why I am a huge fan of her work. Her ability to create witty pieces of writing with a serious undertone is not only clever, it's inspiring. I am always desperately waiting for the next and I forever will for as long as she graces us with her writing!"

- Lauren Honebon, Head of Performing Arts- Manchester Enterprise Academy

"An amazing read, written with honesty and humour making you realise we shouldn't make excuses for who we are. This book had helped me overcome a few inner insecurities. When I'm feeling fragile I always pick up this book and it heals me every time"

- Julia Richards ... Boutique sales person

"What a feast for my eyes, mind and soul. Bindy has a rare gift each piece I read is so honest, raw and true - such a powerful woman.

Just beautifully pure. Thank you"

- Victoria Hyett, Reception manager NHS

"Bindy has a unique technique of highlighting real life issues displaying attitude such as swearing - which we all do in real life situations, but this makes me smile and laugh as her writing is factual, witty and a pleasure to read. No sugar-coating life issues, with Bindy it's the truth. She can hit hard on facts but shows light and humour throughout her work."

- Sharon Jones BA (Hons)- Rehabilitation and prevention professional.

"Real, insightful and emotional with a sharp twist of wit and self-belief, to soften the fabulous delivery of emotive subjects, leaving the reader with a sense of inspiration, empathy and an appreciation of ones self."

- Kellie Hooper, Day Service Officer/ Duty Manager for Generic Day Service.

Foreword.

Hey there!

It's great to meet you. I'd like to introduce you to the author- my amazing, courageous, beautiful, big-haired soul-sister-in-law Bindy Hall.

She has the uncanny ability to "metaphorically kick the seagulls from the rooftops and preach about self worth".

Her words are sharp and uplifting, with a pleasing garnish of humour and bad language on the side.

This book is her in a nutshell.

Just be you xx

Dobby (Deanne) O'Beirne

Contents.

Introduction.

There's enough solidly inspirational and profoundly beautiful literature out there already for your reading pleasure, I won't add to that. Instead I offer you this. I wrote it. I felt compelled to do so because I have a suspicion that, like me, we all worry about and over analyse the same things in life. We are all just anxious meatbags, trying to get along. We all want similar (ish) things. Happiness, family, love, safety, FAME and a metabolism that helpfully speeds up annually on the event of our passing birthdays.

I found this quote a few years ago, it came up as I was scrolling on the internet. It's so beautiful it actually hurts.

"You're a ghost driving a meat coated skeleton, made from stardust. What do you have to be scared of?"

It's deep isn't it? It's basically the theme of this book. It's aim and my intention is to alleviate worries and reassure the reader that we are all the same inside. We ALL relate to the same shit that keeps us awake at night.

I'll be honest... I swear like a trucker, but I sure can write and I have good intentions. And, as the front cover states- it's a guide to surviving the best bits of life and holding our middle fingers up to the rest!

- **Bind**

(Love you Mum!)

B Is For Beautiful.

How many times have you been told you are beautiful? Now, how many times have you shrunk away from the words and felt like they weren't for you? How many times have you been criticised and felt more at ease with this? Why? Why are we more likely to accept that we are flawed than to raise our hands, and say- 'I am beautiful'? Beauty is something we are all in possession of. If you can't find yours, let me help… it's located BEHIND your skin.

If your heart beats and your mind stews, your belly creases when you sit. If your hair grows and your skin protects you… YOU are beautiful! You have survived a shit-tonne of tears and traumas, (yes, shit-tonne is a unit of measurement). You have survived, childhood, heartbreaks, acne, loss, childbirth, (maybe) sleepless nights, interviews, love, marriage, school for 11 years and hangovers from the seventh circle of hell!

If you have overcome life in its many attempts to break or confuse the crap out of you, then I'm here to tell you – you're doing great! Some of us know this and have already plugged into the 'don't hate me cos you ain't me' mentality. Others don't. My mission continues, in space at least, to mentally protect and arm anyone with as much as a teensy-weensy bit of self-doubt, or the kind of confidence that only shows up when the wine does.

Confidence is a muscle, the more you use it the stronger it will become. If you need to rest this 'muscle', imagine every time you go to sleep at night, your self-esteem rests and renews. When you wake up, wake up fierce and ready. You have an invisible layer of protection, you know this because you make it every night, when you sleep. When you step out into the day, you're untouchable. I'm not trying to create any egotistical monsters here; I don't want you all walking about like peacocks with boners! What I hope happens – is that we recognise our worth in all situations.

So, your jeans don't fit, there's just more of you to love and you're harder to kidnap! You're always late for everything, well… it takes time to turn up awesome! When you feel like you can't carry on, look around, see who's watching. When you feel like you have no purpose – remember, somebody, somewhere is looking to you for direction! Lead from the front! YOU will continue to be epic, just believe in yourself.

Oh, you're not everyone's cup of tea. Good! This means you're doing something right. Admiration can breed jealousy. Take these low-key attempts to knock you off your unicorn as a high-five from the universe. You are winning, enough to get on someone else's tits anyway! Other people's opinions of you belong up their arse. You are you and they can deal with it. I'm trying to create a climate of positive change where we support each other to achieve greatness.

Remember Janet from Accounts? Other nemeses are available, *INSERT NAME HERE*, well – she's not too huggable either! The reason the 'Janets' of the world want to hollow you out and use you as storage space for their lip-wax, is because… drumroll… they probably recognise a streak of indomitable gold in you that they haven't yet achieved. Let's help them.

Remember your beauty.

Unwritten.

Unwritten. Is our trajectory or destiny decided for us at birth, or is it all to play for? After all – who better to decide our fate than us? This week I've had a heart wrenching and thought-provoking conversation, with a young lad not much older than my son. He had been verbally squashed and told that he'd either end up in prison or drugged to the eyeballs. This resonated with me straight away. I was told at school by adults in a position of authority and support, that I was useless and shouldn't aim for much. Now you may argue that the motive behind this bullshitty statement, was to evoke a fight back or to spark my teenage motivation. However, I was there. The words, "as much chance of making anything of yourself as snow in hell", said with a vile grin was designed to tread me down.

I know what this lad heard this week and what his heart felt like. Like it had been ironed. I'm certain that we decide our path. What we do and where we end up, is a series of choices. Obviously, there are factors that knock and buffer us off course. Our family, genetics, our personality and largely, sadly, the socio-economic realities that weigh us down like lead pants. With all these things accounted for, I remain resolute that our destiny belongs to us, and is within reach, waiting for us to grab it! This is where the deep-rooted belief that I hold, that we should encourage each other to aim high and be the best version of ourselves comes into play.

There isn't much to be gained from negativity and self-doubt. This is particularly important in the rhetoric we use around our kids.

Their minds and memories are highly absorbent. So... news flash!! If absorbency allows a 'way in', use this entry point to fill their minds with positive encouragement.

Everything we need to win at life is contained within us. We are all of worth. None of us are more primed for success than others. Our future is not at fault due to our beginnings. It is not restricted (permanently at least) by our parents, our looks, our postcode or our shoes.

The key to whether we sink or swim, is a choice. To the kid whose path crossed with mine recently- a message: "Fuck them". Nobody has the right to tell you your limitations, you don't have any.

To the teacher that messed with the teenage me and attempted to put out my anarchist flame, "Fuck you too".

Next month is my graduation, I will have my fabulously supportive husband, and my two amazing kids there to see it. I'm a flower that deserved the water, I blossomed, late – but I got there!

Don't, please don't – let anyone, ever, dim your fucking shine. Your future is beautifully unwritten.

Tits And Arse.

When I was at school, the thing was to have the smallest arse out of everyone. These days, if your butt is the size of a bouncy castle, you're winning. I can't keep up! This is dedicated to a topic very close to my heart, WEIGHT!

Since the age of about ten, I've been aware of how much space I took up. I began to compare myself to other girls. This was obviously normal and a natural thing to do. I'd compare everything, trainers, eye colour, my marble game, (mine was strong by the way) my Afro and most often, my weight. You know when you hit puberty and your body decides you're not fully in charge anymore, oh and here-please accept these e-fucking-normous hips and take them as a down payment on things to come! Well, it was around this beautiful time, that I became obsessed with who in my group of friends was the thinnest, who looked the most athletic, also…why was I the pudgy one?

This dictated for many years to come how many calories I would consume. I learned that I could affect the landscape of my body, by omitting certain food groups. No carbs, low or no fat… just fruit. Bad times. This almost got out of hand around the age of nineteen or twenty, I would force myself to survive on Jolly Ranchers and coffee. Why? No one knows, I think I figured the sweets gave me sugar and energy and the coffee kept me pepped. It had the desired effect anyway, I was soon looking like a pair of eyes on a stick, with some tits thrown in for balance.

Was I happy? No, I was fucking starving and miserable. Plagued with three-day long headaches. The only reward for this self-flagellation was the odd comment, and no, not enough to make my food avoidance endeavours worthwhile.

These days, in my (early) forties the issues around weight are still there, just not in such extremes. I've incorporated a genuine love of running, (I know!) into my body, bingo wing, wobble preoccupation. The running tones up what, if left unattended, would turn to blancmange. My diet could not be healthier, however, age doesn't come alone. Now I can't reliably influence the scales in the direction I want to. My body has now fired me as weight monitor and is fully in the driving seat as to how heavy or light I become. Am I bothered? Thankfully and honestly, I can now say no. It's no longer one of my life goals to have a waist the size of a digestive biscuit. We try to sculpt our physique in a quest to ultimately attract a mate. I don't need to obtain thinness because society or a magazine tells me to. I'm happy with the man I've got, so yes – my edges and corners have softened.

When I see young people punishing themselves for not looking like a perceived ideal, it really worries me. Kids have enough to worry about just getting through their teenage years, without the added pressures of 'does my arse look big enough?' or 'are my arms gunny enough?' Ultimately, you don't gain anything by having the flattest stomach or a thigh gap you could park a Fiat 500 in. What matters is what's going on inside. Be healthy, be kind, be amazing. Be whatever the fuck you like, just don't be defined by your gravitational pull or your fat cell count. I personally blame the likes of Kim K, who ruthlessly airbrushes the selfies she puts on social media, this gives a look that is completely unobtainable. P.S, I saw THOSE pictures of her this week, untouched photos of her on a beach, with an arse like a hippo. If that's what money and the quest for perfection does to you, then I'll avoid if that's OK.

Think of it this way, if we all threw our most maligned body parts or hang-ups into a pile with other people's, we'd see all the others there and gratefully snatch back our own. Appreciate what you have, your heart still beats, doesn't it? Then fuck society and its rules.

Anxiety And Me.

For as long as I can remember, I have not been alone. I have always, since probably playschool, had the company of an ever-present, grey figure beside me. This isn't a ghost story; this spooky mother fucker is anxiety. I feel like I want to share my story in the hopes that other people can relate. They say a problem shared is a problem halved, although, I fear mine is cellular. It's how I'm made. So, let's trace the beginnings of my palm sweat-inducing life chaperone.

I turned up, fuzzy and gobby, into a family already bursting at its seams. In a strong, funny, already established brand of siblings, you better develop a character- quick smart, or…or… I don't know. Sink or swim? Disappear? Or worse, go unnoticed. So, I rolled up my Babygro sleeves and grew a pair of… survival techniques! I probably became brazen and rebellious, before I was ready.

One of my earliest memories was being the only girl at my playschool and giving the boys shit. Deciding who was playing with what toy, and who could join in. I even remember pissing in the boy's toilets standing up! Well, if they could do it, so could I, right? My socks didn't appreciate the warm trickle of amber nectar, that rushed down to meet them. So, I move on to infants' school, we were made to, as I recall anyway, stand in a circle and choose someone to buddy up with. Inappropriate much? Pick a new friend that you like the look of. Based on their appearance? It ends like this- I'm stood there, thinking little shit thoughts, probably with a stick of grass poking out of my hair. There are other kids pairing off all around.

Ooh, two blondies latch on together, cute, whatever. The boys pair off, probably based on their trainers. I continue to stand there, 'fuck you all'… then, it happens. Our eyes lock across the circle of confusion and kid-stink. Two naughty little buggers that each saw in each other, the prospect of future rule breakages. I'd met my first friend, for the sake of privacy, I'll refer to her by her real name, Esther! (you get a mention). So, this is where and when I can actually pinpoint the beginnings of my career as a shitbag.

I've mentioned before that I feel everything; I literally feel everyone's feelings and emotions. Maybe that's why I sometimes shut myself off, as a self-protection thing. While picking up on other people's issues has its benefits, it also has enormous drawbacks. I read on a wall somewhere *'Empathy's great- except you feel sorry for arseholes too'*. True. So, when you feel everyone's joy, you are also susceptible to their beef. Sometimes their feelings towards you aren't so warm and fuzzy. Maybe they think you're a prick.

The general theme of my school years, due to this feeling absorption, was- yes I was smart, but I leaned towards the gobby end of smart. I could NOT take a telling off unless the teller had ten minutes for me to come back at them. Straighten them out, and list all the things that pissed me off about them. This always went down well… I don't know whether it was the innate and utterly profound need in me, to speak out and say my piece, or the societal awareness that I was probably spouting again. But a combination of the two caused an anxiety-induced, see-sawing located specifically around my larynx. I would get so frustrated at an injustice or a shitty unnecessary rule, that the heat and ferocity of my voice would get stifled. Literally choked. I would get tongue-tied to the max, like some bone-dry hand would squeeze my throat, physically shutting me up. I think this was the birth of my anxiety- it was/ is a girl!

I need to be very clear on this point, it's anxiety alone I'm talking about here. Never, thankfully- it's regular dance partner-depression.

Fast forward to present day. I'm opinionated muchly. It's like my opinions have their own opinions, and if they're not aired they'll fester and mutate into weapons grade angst. I've got to express what's what. Any sign of injustice or wrongdoings, I'm literally bent up in anger. This manifestation of anxiousness shows in if I don't want to talk to someone, I can't, or won't. If I do, against my better judgement...shit hits the fan.

I'd rather speak to someone on my terms, than serve up pure sarcasm. The other symptom is, in a room full of people, I can convince myself that NOBODY wants to talk to me. I think I reflect my anxiety onto them, in my head. Parties are particularly fun. Well if they don't want to talk to me, "fuck 'em!", and so, it carries on. The circle of life and societal joy, it's like I developed lead shoes and a chalky tongue. Don't bother striking up conversation Bind, it'll end with you over analysing everything you said within it!

Oh, my goodness, you see? Anxiety is a little grey bitch that I fear is fonder of me than I am if it. Since studying psychology, I now have a better insight into why and how this barrel of emotional bile exists. Brilliant, it doesn't however, stop it.

I've found an amazingly therapeutic outlet that seems to be acting like a sugar-coated anxiety pill. I now write, I have to. I get a build-up of what I want to say. It's such a literal build up, that I feel like I want to puke it out. I grab a pen and paper and get to work. When I've allowed it out, it's like bloodletting in ink form. I feel a release, like the feeling of nausea that's relieved by your visit to the big, white trombone. Instantly better. I appreciate my readers, really. I've said it before I hope to create a reader community of likeminded humans. We all take a knock now and again on life's path.

For me, as I've already said, my life is fun and beautiful, but I guess you've got to have something, right? It can't all be plain sailing.

Chin up folks, we're all the same on the inside.

The Waiting Room.

Dementia, as I hear on an all too regular basis is a particularly cruel and heart-wrenching disease. It creeps up on its victim like a thief in the night. It can slowly chew away at your once brilliant relative and leave them confused, scared, forgetful or aggressive, amongst many other symptoms. How is this fair and why should we tolerate it?

Lately, somebody very close to me has been undergoing some changes. I'm trying to be polite here… At first, you can attribute these subtle anomalies to the fact that we're all human, we all have good and bad days, stress can play tricks with our memory, right? I've tried to brush off the impending doom of what might really be happening here, but I'm not too sure how successful this will ultimately be.

As with anything like this, us folk do like to seek out others going through the same or similar situations. I've spoken to a few people who are currently, helplessly being forced to watch, as the inevitability of this foul condition unfolds and their loved one mentally wanders off into the unknown, leaving a look-a-like shell behind.

I knew I wanted to write something on the subject of dementia, as always, the reasons for my writing- (other than self-help/ therapy), is to fire out pockets of help into cyberspace. If even one person gets a chink of comfort from my thoughts, I'll be happy.

I've given this topic a lot of attention, I've read a lot of articles on Alzheimer's, Lewy bodies dementia, Parkinson's disease, even autism. I read too much! Instead of getting all scientific, I decided to concentrate on MY take on it. DISCLAIMER!! Just so you know, this is only my take, I tend to see things a little alternatively as I think I register fairly high on the autistic spectrum, (just a hunch). If you scream and shout in disagreement with it, that's your thing, not mine. The common ground I hope we'll all have, is that indeed, dementia is an utter shit. Always has been, always will be.

So, my experiences of this disease comes from two stellar ladies in my family and a man I met in a care home years ago, whose tears and ramblings will probably stay with me forever. Heartbreaking! Everyone is so quick and rightly so, to say how unfair and devastating dementia is. Obviously, I'm not on the side of this memory thief, this isn't a defence plea on its behalf. I just need to regain autonomy over my despair I guess…

Dementia literally steals the light from a person's eyes. You see them forgetting the most beautiful parts of their lives. Their children, how could they forget their own children? Their husband/ wife, how after 45 years of sleeping next to somebody, can they misplace their memories of them? It's so cruel, so heart snapping. This disease doesn't respect intelligence levels either, it doesn't matter if they were, 'always so bright'. Tough, the rules are clear, it will have full memory wiping privileges with your mum or dad's brain. It will take your once independent, loving, funny parent and empty out all these qualities. Not all at once, no, no… one at a time while you are forced to watch from behind a glass panel, without popcorn! Hideous. What an utterly unjust finale to such an important and sparkling life.

My view on this has formed with the conversations I've had with the sufferers themselves. In the early stages, they are aware of what they have forgotten. Their pin or phone number. A name to a face. Maybe they forgot your birthday? They'll become frustrated and fearful of the future. What else will they forget? To go to the toilet? Where they live? Their grandchildren? Their still conscious thoughts run wild with the uncertainty that is rolling out before them.

I've tried to offer reassurance in this situation. The one thing I can be certain of is this; dementia is a million times more heartbreaking for the observer than the sufferer. I've joked and said, "It's alright for you, it'll be us that'll deal with it". I joke but it's true. The more I think about it, the more I have to get a different view on the injustice of it. Yes, dementia is a disgrace. One of the worst fates anyone can suffer, but also in my need to comprehend and reason with it, I have chosen to look for a freebie beam of light. One that will ensure I cope with what the future brings.

What if dementia is a waiting room? A stop off on route to our final destination. What if, this waiting room takes the awareness of the symptoms or the inevitability of death and keeps them away from the sufferer? Like a neurological barrier or protective force. Maybe they deserve to be unaware of the sadness around them. Spared. Yes, for the family, watching their loved one deteriorate will be devastating, they will feel helpless and frustrated at being unable to do anything.

For the sufferer themselves, they are being spared the enormity of their fate. Comfortably numb. If you are getting annoyed now in disagreement, stay with me- I haven't finished! Even if on the surface they are distressed or aggressive. The spirit of their younger, healthier self has taken a comfortable seat in this waiting room between two worlds. The conscious part of their brain has pulled up anchor and sailed off. The two ladies mentioned earlier, are so profoundly golden that they deserve to be anything but aware as they succumb to their fate.

Somewhere in their cerebral cortex, they are dancing on the shiniest of floors in the most beautiful dresses they have ever owned. The waiting room is a first edition heaven, where they wait and revisit all the beautiful memories made in their lives. They stay seated here until the second edition comes out.

Wouldn't you like to be mentally, 'not in' when Death came calling for you? There's some poetic justice in that surely?

"Is she in?"

"No, fuck off – she's already left."

Ticket To Anywhere.

Life. The magic and fragility of it have become even more vividly apparent in the last couple of months. Our extended family are three members down. Also, the cutest, most idiotic and loving dog, a dog that cared for my children – almost as much as I did, became sick and left us. He got his furry wings and buggered off, leaving me and mine to deal with the fallout.

We could – and obviously do, sit and lament over their losses. As humans, we are pack animals. We mourn so painfully the loss of our loved ones. But what if we change our perspective? What if the person who has left us hasn't really gone anywhere? All that happens is that they are, for now, gone from view. They are still nearby, within touching distance, we just can't see them. I don't imagine them in an ethereal way, covered in glitter, with a halo made of a bent-up coat hanger. If black leather or a football strip was their thing, then that is how they remain, eternally.

Lately, I have felt the gap between this life and the next getting smaller. This is a great source of comfort as well as a huge relief to my mascara! Firstly, my brother lost his wife. Unfortunately, he didn't misplace her, she was taken far too young and devastated him by dying. The strength that he has found since this happened and the way he has adapted to his new life sans partner, has been amazing. The loss will never leave him, obviously – but he knows that she is free from the pain of the cancer that took her. She has a ticket to anywhere, she will use it beautifully. Collecting heavenly air miles whilst always being a heartbeat away from her husband, if, and when he needs her.

We've had two further losses since, one was my Auntie, who had had her life, it was her time to rest. Even though this was less traumatic than when a young person is snatched away, her family are still feeling the loss that not having her around will leave. I positively and without any doubt – know that my Granddad, Charlie would have come to escort his girl over the bridge… he would have held out his fatherly hand and pulled her to her new safety. Guess how I know this? I'm so sure of the link between heaven and earth, because I would have to be killed twice before I left my kids. I would literally wrestle a lion to keep them safe, and I know that won't stop when I die. A maternal bond is too strong to be broken by a little cellular deficit. I'll be there for them always, they'll feel a supportive hand on their back when they need me. I'll turn up at family get-togethers and eat invisible vegan food and sup on otherworldly Tia Marias and coke.

I remember once, I had been really poorly, I had a virus and had been awake all night. I got up to go to the loo and fainted. As I fell and as my shoulder absorbed the impact of the landing floor, my last thought was, 'are my kids OK?' Weirdly, as I came round again, I caught the tail end of this worry, were they OK? This is the indelibleness of my love. It cannot be removed.

This piece wasn't intended to be sad, so here is some golden proof of a mother's love transcending boundaries of death. My sister, who passed away 22 years ago, was at the wedding of her youngest child, this week! I knew there would be an extra guest there. It makes sense, doesn't it? If she is in spirit and has her ticket to anywhere, why wouldn't she go over to Cyprus and watch her boy get married? Evidence of this came from the mouth of her tiny granddaughter, who had an encounter with 'the lady with the curly hair', when there was nobody around her. When questioned on whether she had seen this lady before, she said 'yes, I see her at home too'. Then pointed her out in an old photo.

I recently had a reading with a couple of mediums. They told me what I already knew, that my Granddad looks out for me and mine. He had a message for me, he said, 'heaven is beautiful, and we'll all be together one day'. He also told me to look out for robins, as he sends them to me. This guy never met me, he was born in 1900 and died before I was born, yet he is still influencing things in the land of the living.

He's been busy lately, meeting people at the gate. Well Granddad, look after Derek dog, throw the ball just how he likes it.

It's written somewhere special… memories are like a golden chain that bind us until we meet again.

Fuck you Death, you hit like a bitch.

Sorry Not Sorry.

Food for thought; why do we apologise so much? What makes us, as individual entities feel the need to say, 'sorry', for shit that's not our fault? When somebody bumps into us, we say it. When plans don't pan out because of the Englishness of the weather, we are quick to offer up a 'sorry', almost as a knee jerk, unthought through, drummed in from birth reaction. Why?

Feeling obliged to apologise for shit we aren't personally responsible for, stems from insecurity. We all have insecurities, even those of us who think we're Teflon coated. *My passport photo here.* I've apologised for such weird things over the years, it's untrue. My hair, the way I talk, being too pissed, forgetting to show up…. I genuinely didn't want to go! I think I get this from my mum, who in turn, probably unknowingly inhaled it from her post-war childhood. Sorry for wanting something different, sorry there isn't more of this, sorry if I'm still hungry, etc.

She still does this now. If I tell her I hate my job- she immediately, without batting an eye, dispenses a 'sorry love'. It's like an out of hours email response. This person is not responsible for your shitty life choices, but in an attempt to placate your whinging face, I offer you my apologies. I'm back in the office tomorrow. Now, I understand why she does this, she's a fixer- she wants to fix everything for everyone. But in doing this, she has passed on this indelible, reflexive habit to me.

All is not lost, the purpose of my writing is to challenge the issues that have a negative impact on our lives. In an attempt to stamp out this tendency for over-owning shit, I have developed a new habit that beats the crap out of the old one. Firstly, we can simply say, 'fuck you'. I know, my favourite phrase. I'm having it iced on to my next birthday cake! This, you got in my way, you got yourself into that, kind of approach, can and does work, but it's basic and has its limitations, also it can leave a bruise on your conscience.

The best advice I have on this matter, is to switch up the wording of our responses. Add a positive twist. Instead of saying, 'I'm sorry I'm late' replace this with, 'thank you for being patient'. An alternative to apologising that you've gained some Christmas chub, suggest that people should be grateful that you are now easier to find. When you're leaning towards saying something self-deprecating, 'I'm so scatty, I'm such a pain in the arse, I'm too...' anything. Take a breath, instead say, 'thanks for loving me just how I am'. This covers most things, even my messy cupboard affliction, poor Nath!

Lately, I've been putting some of my own choices and ways under scrutiny. I left a safe job to venture out looking for something more challenging. Good work, eh? Only, the new job was so structured, so regimented, so...not me. It got so bad, I started to question what was wrong with me. Then, reliably I should have known, my soul starts poking me from inside my heart. She was like, 'Pssst! Hey, you, you fucking hate this job don't you?' I sit there developing a thought, worthy of my fourteen-year-old self. I figured if I got my bag and coat and drove straight home. I could be watching Only Fools and

Horses in twenty minutes. So, I get up. I say fuck it to the regime that was upsetting my flow and I freed myself!!

Now, am I sorry? No. I see it as – I looked after me, I bought to an end a situation that was thoroughly chaffing on my wellbeing, so no – I'M NOT SORRY!

Also, I've had it pointed out that I'm selectively friendly. This is incorrect and something else I'm not sorry for. My vibe attracts my tribe. If we don't vibe, I don't sweat it. Friendship, as I understand it is based on a mutual appreciation of another's awesomeness. A shared sense of humour, a natural ability to build each other up and an aggressive belief in each other. If I'm too salty for you, I'm not sorry, but I do hope your luck improves.

I'm not averse to being sorry, I just believe that when we apologise, we should mean it and take ownership over what we are saying sorry for.

So be done with the, throw away, ten times a day, apologising for inane shit. A by-product of this new, think before we sink attitude, comes a new season of collectable, growing confidence.

I'll leave you with this thought, if you are about to take the blame for a situation that is not of your making, push it away. After all, there are a million words more fun to say than, 'sorry'.

Try, 'up yours', I guarantee you'll smile soon afterwards.

Vibes.

Trusting ourselves and learning to listen to our gut, has got to be held up and framed as a target. A lifelong, reliable working progress. Honed as a personal, easily accessible, largely infallible google.

This offering, circles around the subject of innate intuition, and why we should respect the hell out of it.

So, I've had a bit of a hiatus since I last wrote. Stuff happens I guess, stuff that occupies my time and detracts from the newly prominent, writer's bureau in my right hemisphere. I had started to write on the topic of intuition and instinct. I'm always fascinated by the way my belly reacts to people I come across, or situations I find myself in.

My writing was taking shape, around the other stuff that keeps me upright during the day. Anyway, I became briefly distracted. I had a couple of chances to write for some big websites. Get published? Get paid? I got a bit excited. I started to wonder why JK Rowling dropped out of the Forbes 100 list. Worse problems to have...

During these emailed convos, I was faintly aware of a little nagging doubt in the background, trying to burst my bubble. It was a tiny version of me, sensible shoes and no hair products- sat on my shoulder. She was saying, "Bind- you don't need to sell out. Stay raw, you know you love your Fuck- its". The other shoulder had a blinged up, afro'ed version dollar sign round her neck. Rapping something about- making bank?! Twat!

Fast forward two weeks. Seems like my initial instincts were bang on. The outcome of my 'big breaks' were; one of the editors said they loved my stuff, they thought it was marketable- but could I tone down the language, as I came off a little aggressive! Me? Aggressive? How fucking dare... Um no. I love swearing. The swearing stays.

The other, long conversations with a REALLY young editor, he loved my stuff and was complimentary, my content was relatable, and other mild-mannered pronouns. However, and this was the ball breaker- they wouldn't use any of my stuff, they would give me topics to write about each week.

Say what?? Well, paint me red! So, hang on... would I have to change my name to Howard Handupme? I get to fall in line and get paid in the form of a creative lobotomy? And that's when I thought, you know what? Fuck it. Fuck it and fuck you.

I've only just discovered my writing thing, it's new to me. I love it! I need it, it's my favourite thing to do with a pen. I like waking up at 3:00 am with a paragraph trying to eek its way out of my brain. It's an extension of my soul, why would I surrender it up to someone else? I've always been resistant to conformity, that's not about to change.

So why didn't I listen to my initial intuition? I'm usually unapologetic, if something's fucky - I'll say so. I guess we live and learn. Also, it's perfect material for the topic.

So, why do we question ourselves? I sometimes feel bad about catching a vibe from someone. I'll meet people who are so, 'not for me', it's like they're luminous. I'll get a, 'no- not feeling it'. The rational part of me convinces me to give them a chance, because it's not great to pre-judge. Later something confirms my suspicions and they turn out to be a melon baller, (scoops out your good bits and leaves you for dead). Round of applause intuition, you tried to warn me.

On the flip side, there are people- who, after two minutes of talking to them, my face is beaming. It's like 'hello old friend, where were you?' I catch this vibe too, something is telling me 'go on, this one's for you, you're welcome'. Vibes don't lie.

I said there would be homework with this edition. Firstly, I want you to listen to your gut. When you get a choice to go one way or another, silence yourself. Just listen, sometimes it's audible. You'll get a little lurch in your belly, saying 'no, not that way- this way'. Go with that.

When you get invited somewhere and you really don't want to go. Don't feel obliged, just give thanks and decline. Protect your space. You go to get in a taxi, on your own, or in a lift. It's just going to be you and one other; you catch a negative whiff. Step back, just say thanks and walk away. Your intuition is alerting you to something or someone it has reservations about. Welcome this as free advice.

Instincts are there for a reason, to protect. They are primitive and innate. Think of it like this, even if you haven't been fully aware of all our past experiences, your gut has been taking notes. It's got a filing cabinet full of them and now recognises good and bad shit before we are even aware. That's why it shouts to warn us. We just have to listen.

The next time you find yourself in a shitty situation that you don't fully love. Listen to your intuition, get the hell out of there, and remember what your middle finger is for.

Jigsaw Heart.

Learn her.

Learn what unlocks her soul.

Respect her fragile strength.

Learn the quirky little things that illuminate her smile.

Notice when worry shows up, etched into the flower shop window - that is her face.

Recognise when she feels alone, redundant, or not enough.

Appreciate her hungry mind, she is still becoming...

Feel pride in the enormity of the love she has for her children, be aware that they are pieces of her jigsaw heart and they and will always be what completes her.

Read the books that nourish her thoughts, they will help you see the world from her private angle.

Compliment her uncertain beauty, there will only ever be one 'now'.

Today she is the best version of herself, don't put off enjoying her until tomorrow, it may never come.

Put her first, think of her always. Be worthy.

Envelope her in protective, iron wings.

Trace the edges of her soul with your fingers and recognise the implicit beauty contained within.

Remember her smile so that you can find it in a sea of others.

Keep your word, broken promises leave bruises on the heart.

Learn her...

Love her.

Leave an imprint on her soul that will last into the next life.

If you love her right... she will find you again, in heaven.

Handle With Care.

Handle with care and I don't just mean when you find yourself in the glassware section of Debenhams. I mean people's hearts. We're all guilty of maybe, not meaning to, but sometimes giving half a shit about others, whether it's taking a week to respond to a text, or not knowing what to say when hearing someone's bad news... 'My goldfish died', 'oh really? I've got to go; I'm getting my eyebrows done'. This, this is the shit I'm talking about. The not really bothered about your shit, shit. So, this has been written as a handy cut out and keep guide, to looking after the feelings of others. To be a better helper, one whose sincerity reaches out further than an inch away from your body.

So, you'll know from my previous writings, which are basically just internal ramblings of my avant-garde mind, that I metaphorically kick the seagulls from the rooftops and preach about self-worth. This offering aims to explain why and shine a light on the origins of my life remit. It stems from a sink or swim, notice yourself or go unnoticed, kind of deal.

I spent years being the fuzzy, awkward, hand-me-down skinny kid. I eventually twigged, that if I wanted to survive as anything other than a P.S or a footnote, I'd have to step out of my shy shoes and cultivate my own brand of life.

I realised my importance and wore (wear) it like a statement Tee. It was this or a life of banality and only mild fun! Nah... That's why I chose to become professional with the profanity and developed a 'fuck you, I'm fine' attitude. Get it? If this is ever perceived as cocky, then good. Join me, hello new friend!

You'll understand then that we all have reasons why we are who we are. There are traceable paths to explain our personality traits. Mine was a survival tool that became my shining life mantra. My crown is now the prefix to my name. Because I spent a while unsure of my lovableness, then found it, I still have a residual trace of bruiseability left behind. Like a footprint on my wing. My surface will remain flexed, but my heart will hoover up any sign that someone's not interested in me or what I've got to say. I get this a lot. Folks will say, 'Hi' and chat to Nath, and then at the last minute- I get an… 'oh, hi'. Sometimes I don't even get that. Nath will say, "Shit they didn't even notice you!" I'm like, "Oh, you noticed that?"

I am hard-wired to pick up on when I'm talking to someone and I see their eyes notice someone else behind me, and then it's, "Yeah, yeah - I've got to go". Go about your business, only stop to speak if you want to, I'm not an obligation, I'm a soul. This influences me when I deal with other people. We never know what they are dealing with or why. You can't, just by looking begin to imagine the shit that a person has had to contend with or has lived through. Maybe it has left them angry, or rude or untrusting. Maybe too trusty and eager to please, vulnerable. Maybe they overcompensate in their behaviour, spend too much, drink too many, or love inappropriately.

I would like us all to take these factors into account when judging or interpreting the people we engage with. Give a shit, ask how they are. Compliment but not just on their appearance. Notice when someone has done really well and achieved, tell them they rock! Celebrate their uniqueness as well as your own. Praise them but mean it. Don't notice, the negative points, notice their smile or the great job they're doing with their kids or their life!

Be aware that if they look a little sad, they may need you to hear them or make them smile. If they begin to tell you a little about their stuff, don't look at your phone or change the subject. They are sharing a little of themselves and need you to show humanity. It really is the little things, a callback, a compliment or just be a complete twat and make them laugh.

My absolute pet hate is when someone asks me how I am, or how my kids are doing. I'll think, oh OK... they must want to know, or why would they ask? So, I start to get animated, my kids are my favourite topic... then I get, 'sorry- I've got to get going'. So don't fucking ask me then. That really busts my arse.

My other little personal need is, I have to FEEL like I'm actually needed or wanted. Don't get all psycho-babble on me. This isn't a sign that I'm needy, I just mean - say, for instance, you invite me somewhere. The invite has to be golden, you can't just say 'we're having a get-together, pop in if you like'. I need a firm, 'I want you at this event' or I don't come. I don't do flaky stuff, I have to feel it. This is what remains from the unsure of my self-stage of my life.

I'm pretty sure we are fundamentally the same, we all have feelings, we all need love. We all need to belong and to feel of value. Basically, treat people the way you would like to be treated. A lot of the mental health crisis that we see on the news, could at least be helped, if we all took exceptional care of our own people. Of our own family. The ones in your life. Look after them- fully. Don't let them fall through the cracks, people aren't disposable. We are all fighting a fight, some of us fight alone- others need a hand.

Be the best, kindest version of yourself and never leave anyone behind.

The Best Things In Life Aren't Things.

Today is my birthday, I am forty- fucking- one! How is this possible? It only seems like a couple of years ago, I was basking in the glow of the turd I'd just made on the potty. Now what? Bills and a weak bladder? How? How am I now four decades plus one? I guess grey hairs, stretch marks, a weird draw towards comfy shoes... cardigans. All these things are an inevitable attribute to the passage of time.

I'd like to feel pissed off at the young me, the one that flounced off into the vaults of my memory, wearing Fila trainers and sass. The size eight- Afro'd me, has been replaced by a rounder, nuttier woman. One that likes floral prints (what the fuck?) I now get off on Spanx and vitamins, this shit would not have been tolerated twenty years ago! Jesus. But instead of feeling cheated or freaked out by this finger-snap time elapse, I feel like I want to lay out on a table and admire all that I have now. Lay it out and smile a massive hormone induced smile.

Time, with its rapid drive-by, has bought me many, MANY gifts. Pull up a chair, this may take a while. OK, so if I'm contrasting or comparing the younger me to today's birthday girl, let's start with the doozy, the big one - LOVE. These days I don't question whether I'm enough, I don't wonder about my lovableness. The love I get from him indoors is strong and protective. It's iron-clad. Nath's got my back and I've got his. So that flappy section of my temporal lobe has relaxed onto a velvet chaise lounge of contentedness. Would I want to swap this for a teenage, angst-ridden search for affection? Um ... ...no!

Next up, tits and err... the rest of me. Activate memory vision. Remember your teenage tits and arse, you got it? Remember the smooth lines and the nips you could use to find north if you were lost? Were you happier? Was I? No, I bloody wasn't. My award winning tits and unconcerned butt of old, spent the best part of eighteen hours a day on lockdown anyway. What was the 'point' of them? The sitch is the same now, thanks to nudity laws, ergo, who gives a fuck if my lady lumps are spaniels-ears-esque in their forties? Nobody, that's who.

With age comes a surety and degree of chilledness that a younger me would have killed for. Back then I would have apologised for looking like shit or for gaining a couple of pounds. The 'me' me, with the extra few rings of time hung around my neck, suggests that you look away if you don't like what you see. Keep walking mother fucker. Ha! I fucking love being this age. My philosophy these days is- if you don't like it, tough shit! Who wouldn't prefer this age-induced, firming up and removal of their insecurities?

Another big life concern that hid under my fully brown, (no grey bits) barnet, was what would I do in life, what would I become, how would I direct my aimless, skinny self? Fast forward... and aww nice, I've found my niche and earned my place there. I'm no longer directionless and "seriously considering becoming an astronaut".

But you know what the biggest lesson I've learned is? The best things in life aren't things. They aren't the possessions we collect on the way. They aren't the achievements of whatever we've done, to pat ourselves on the back. They're not even the home we make or the car we drive. The best bits about life are the people we share it with. People are my thing; I didn't realise their enormous value until the second I became a mother. In that magical, painful epiphany-EVERYTHING became clear. It was like the path in front of me, flattened out and developed road markings and signs. My anxieties and lack of direction were thrown out with the afterbirth. Direction, purpose, endless love and the maternal instincts of a lactating lioness. This was my new gig.

I knew then that the best things in life were not things. The best bits about life accumulate over time. As time elapses, you watch your children grow and learn, mine have turned into two of the best humans I have ever met. We experience life at its best and worst, every stage is a valuable lesson that we can pass on to our kids. I have let go of the consuming grip of the importance of wrinkle-free face or a reliable bladder. My new desires involve happy offspring, a clean loo seat and low cholesterol!

As I turn forty-one, I'm chilled out completely to my core. Getting older is a privilege denied to many. Too many. I feel lucky to be upright, healthy and above ground. How lucky am I? Yesterday I was forty, today I'm forty-one, hopefully, it slows down a bit then and forty-two is a year away.

Bring on the wrinkles, today I'll eat cake in celebration of life, love and the benefits of a good moisturiser.

Label Jars Not People.

I am a... Mum, wife, sister, writer, sandwich artiste, daughter, laundry negotiator and rum connoisseur. But I am much more than this. I am a sum of my parts, we all are. We all develop skills to help us get by. And, we are all still becoming.

I want to know why we are so intent on defining people with a label or by their job title. I've noticed lately during my ' I hate this job, let's add to my hairnets and name tags,' phase, that folk are very interested in what job I'm going for. What's the pay scale? What's the job title? How about ask me if I'm happy? Why not ask what happened at the last job? My last two jobs could have continued around a cardboard cut-out of me without anyone noticing. There would have been less swearing and more coffee left over- but that's about it. Me being an existential thinker, questioned this before ducking out and fucking off.

My place in life is in a therapeutic role, I'm on the last stretch of training to be able to counsel others. Part of this involves being counselled. Holy fuck! The mind debris this brings up. If I leave a thin layer of snot on you after we've spoken I apologise, buts it's all for the cause. When I'm done I'll acquire a new label. Amongst familial law enforcer, sleep hunter and provider of fine (frozen) foods, I'll add in therapist. I'll be verified by my new title, right?

That depends, do I need to feel like I'm verified, approved of? Do any of us. Our self-worth should come from inside, from how we feel about ourselves. I hear people mentally peeling off a fresh sticker, ready to apply to anyone who's a bit different. Maybe this one's a single mum, this one's got mental health issues, she's fat, she's too thin. He's unemployed. I guess they help with the sorting process. I think labels can be damaging and impose limitations on people. Labels are dependent on someone else's point of view. What the?!... How you define yourself is what really counts. Fuck labels, am I right?

I was in the supermarket the other day, the girl on the checkout was chatting to me. She said, although she quite liked her job, she wanted to study to do something else. She said she wanted her kids to be proud, and that checkout girl wasn't particularly a reason for them to feel pride. Then she laughed and said, "But I can't- I'm too stupid!"

I nearly filled up. "Say what?"

I asked her who told her she was stupid, she just changed the subject and instead commented on my magazine. I couldn't stop thinking about that girl, she's been made to believe that she's not capable of much, how damaging and unnecessarily bloody limiting! I FUCKING HATE THIS! Her self-worth had come from somebody else's, flawed opinion. She seemed epic, holding down a job to pay her bills, raising her kids and surviving. She's capable of anything - but also, just as importantly- nothing! She/we are capable of massive things, but do we all have to strive for a new milestone?

There's a shit load of rhetoric around maximising potential, aiming high and achieving great things. How about we first accomplish the label of 'happy'? In the scramble to 'be' something worthwhile, I feel like we forget the importance of mental wellness. Let's aim for a label of good, happy, healthy human. We should appreciate the jobs we do that are never ending accomplishments in their own rights. The jobs we do that get shit done, every, single, day! What job role do you know that requires you to do all the unpaid stuff that you do? The cleaning, getting puked on, teacher, chef, advisor, defender, shirt-ironer and taxi. How about you add to that list, 'hero' and leave yourself time to smile. I think we should start a campaign to appreciate the jobs we already do, without the pressure to climb any professional ladders. How about we realise that we have already accomplished a lot and if today all you managed to do was survive, then I have a label ready and waiting for you. It says 'Champion,' I hope you like it.

So, if self-worth comes from the boxes that people define you into, take a look down this list. Count how many you do, unsalaried, without thinking and because you're fabulous:

1. Mum
2. Dad
3. Sister/brother
4. Friend
5. Supporter
6. CEO of the household
7. Personal chauffeur

8. Appointment clerk
9. Doll doctor
10. Spiritual and development guide
11. Medication reminder
12. Odd sock hunter (fuck sake)
13. Celery avoider
14. Keeper of secrets
15. Birthday cake maker
16. Dog walker
17. Finance manager
18. Shopper
19. Supplier of assorted sandwiches
20. All round legend.

Do you feel verified yet?

Fuck the negative categorising of people.

We are enough.

I Am You.

Confession/ realisation:

I am my own worst enemy.

I'm the reason I cannot sleep.

I'm what's holding me back.

I'm the reason you worry.

I'm the one that you explain to others.

I starve myself only to binge later.

I'm the early hours.

I'm the empty coffee jar.

I'm your zero bank balance.

I overthink as a sport.

I definitely teach kids to swear (they learn it sooner or later!).

I miss the mark.

I avoid the difficult bits.

I don't give way.

I wear sunglasses to hide my tears.

I don't need love but need all of it.

I am too much but never enough.

I sweep stuff under the carpet.

I have to relearn lessons that I thought I had bagged.

I fail, I trip, I scream.

I am faulty.

BUT THEN AGAIN...

I rebuild.

I stand tall.

I shower off the losses and reapply the wins.

I am resilient.

I love you to the fucking moon and back.

I am my ancestors' best intentions.

I was born ready.

I am my own place of safety.

I can overcome.

I remember my worth.

I am capable of remarkable achievements.

I will never leave you.

I dry my own tears and cheer myself on.

I am the proof.

I will blossom.

Watch me though, because...

I AM YOU.

Roots And Wings.

You know, they say that empty nest syndrome is merely a feeling of grief and loneliness that we parents experience. It's not a psychological or medical condition or anything above a neuroticism. Oh, that's good. Just feelings huh? Here's my issue though; don't we run on our feelings, our emotions? How we feel - can't for any length of time, be put away in a cupboard so we don't have to deal with it. This period of transition- for a while at least, will become the new norm. So, I need to look at it.

At this time in my life and that of many friends and people I know, our children have grown up. We've carefully and lovingly kept them safe. I was/ am obsessively conscious of anything that posed a threat to my two children. Be it illness, other kids, lost toys, hunger, the bastard bogey man... anything that got close to the vicinity of mildly pissing off my best assets, I was ready for. Put 'em up, bitches! I'm by no means unique. I've been doing some research, not that it was needed. Most mothers worth their salt, if you ask them, will tell you. They love their children so entirely, so unconditionally, that if their uterus has served them correctly- their offspring's needs more than wholly take precedence over any remnant of self-requirements.

I have been a mother for a quarter of a century, (yes I dye my hair). Twenty-five years is a long time, enough to change self-serving habits, to re-route neural pathways and fundamentally to enforce the laws of light sleep. Those times your mini humans had accepted and completed the McDonald's challenge, before barfing up and sleeping! My trick for staying awake or at least making sure I woke up to check on my two when they were poorly involved my bladder. Old reliable I call it. I'd glug a pint of cold water before climbing the wooden hill, knowing that if I did manage to fall asleep, I'd need a wee in the small hours. This meant I'd join the wide awake club, long enough to check on my cubs. Job done! Of course, there was always a risk that I'd pee the bed, but it never happened.

After all of this, habit forming, thought changing time that we expend to our kids. How was it ever going to be easy for us to be suddenly redundant? Shut off. Surplus to requirements. Is it any wonder then, that when our kids move on, venture out or go off to Uni, we feel such a palpable sense of grief and despair?

Who will we check on ten times a day? Will they be OK? What if they're hungry? My personal favourite- what if somebody gives them shit, speaks to them badly or takes the piss? I want to help, that's my job, right? Then there's the empty bedroom. The foods they like that you buy, let go out of date then re-buy, just in case. AND WHAT ABOUT MY HEART?

I met a friend for coffee the other day, as we sat deciding which one was coconut milk and which was cow's, she told me how empty nest syndrome had affected her. Her obviously and utterly precious son going off to Uni had left behind a tsunami of emotions. She was stoked with pride at the same time as filled with grief. She described it as like a bereavement, only into this quagmire of sadness she felt the added complication of guilt. Relief covered guilt if you will. Her son was alive and well- just not where she could see him. What compounded her feelings was that she knew of a family that had suffered the actual loss of their young child and here she was, feeling the 'loss' of her very healthy son.

The feelings of an empty nest and the relentless build-up of 'mothering' that continues to form inside of you, is visceral. It's real. A tangible nod to the amazing work we have done over the years. A theme to my writing is wanting to analyse and challenge our perspectives. I take ENS as a sign that we've done alright thank you very much!

If we've completed our mission and held our children's hands, negotiating them through childhood. Successfully raising good humans, then yes, we will and should feel the loss that their sporadic presence will bring.

My suggestion for this is to, as my kids would say, 'get out more, Mum.' We should take this time to focus and regroup. Meet friends for coffee, join a gym, read my book, pop bottles at the weekend. Use the time to relax into the next stage of your life. If we've done it right, our kids will be resilient and learn to thrive outside of the nest, even if they do bring their washing home sometimes.

They know where we are should they need us, until then just remember; there are two gifts we should give our children, one is roots the other is wings.

Fuck It Up Buttercup.

Rejoice! I've got another issue for you to mull over. One more item to add to the list of life perplexers, existential ailments and reasons to ask ourselves, 'what the fucking fuck?' twenty times a fricking day: - SELF SABOTAGE.

You know what I mean, I know you do this too, I'm talking about the inexplicable patterns of behaviour that we pull from nowhere, right when we DON'T need them. It's as if we're bored of everything going our way. Life is flat, tidy and polite. We need to (subconsciously) pull the rug out from underneath our own feet! In my case, I am certain that my guardian angel has a booze problem, gets drunk and starts fights with me! Thanks love.

Let me give you some of my own examples:

I had an interview the other day, I'd prepped my Q and A's, updated my CV and got there in plenty of time. The meeting was going quite well, I begin laying out my stall as it were. We get half an hour into it. Then it happens, the bored, up-for-a-challenge part of my brain, decides it's got a new plan! Apparently, the interview needed some spice. My mouth starts drying up and my palms start to sweat, all pretty innocuous... until I hear random words coming out of my mouth, like 'microwave' and 'nimbus cloud'. Nice, cheers brain. I certainly love you.

It's as if a part of my self is intent on stopping me shoot for the moon and has instead taken aim at my temple. I've read up about this, its perceived fraudulence. In a nutshell, I got my qualifications later in life. My mindset hasn't evolved much from the fuzzy kid that wasn't on track to achieve squat. I know this, which is why I find myself here, languishing in this fourth paragraph. My rusty cognition hasn't yet caught up.

So that covers the interview madness for now. But, can someone please explain why I had an 'incident', with sugar-free sweets the other day? Sugar-free eh? Where's the harm? There is no harm until I nearly shit myself driving home from work from all the Xylitol that I knew I was allergic to. Why in the name of Stevie Wonder - would I knowingly, as a functioning adult do that?? Beats the shit out of me, literally it's like the usually dormant self-destruct button presses itself; I fucking swear!

Lastly, and this one's the chubbiest of all the examples. I do this really odd thing, where I'll be preparing for an event, a holiday or a wedding. I lay off the carbs and drink loads of water, I get my hair done. I'm feeling good, my tummy flattens out so much that my ironing board gets jealous and Fucks off! My outfit is going to look banging. Then, for no other reason than the thought of it slowly tiptoed through my mind, I decide to set myself a challenge on how much bread I can actually eat in one day!! Great, now here comes the bloat! I look down, it's as if my fat cells have promoted themselves, they are now holding hands in a friendship group around my belly button.

Brilliant.

Self-sabotage for me, unconsciously creates a fleeting, familiar feeling of mild chaos. Now that feeling is something I do know how to react to, I just need to remind myself not to take a chainsaw to the branch I'm sitting on.

I offer this collection of words up to the gods of 'sorting out our shit.' I'm hoping that now I've put it into writing, it'll serve as a reminder to myself and others that we're definitely worth better than this. So, be prepared. Recognise those crumbs of self-sabotage before they escalate into the whole belly bloating loaf.

As ever, I strive onwards and upwards.

I'm off to eat a vegan ice cream. Why? Because I'm on a diet - obviously.

Dear Younger Me.

OK, where do I start?

The good news is, spoiler alert - YOU MAKE IT! I just wanted to clear that up straight away. Amazing stuff happens. Love finds you, (I know, you weren't lost). You meet a human that is the other half of your soul, not that you were ever anything but whole alone.

You have two kids, who change your LIFE. Watch them though, they're supersonic. They will fill your heart with love in the heaviest of doses. You will feel pride like you didn't know was possible and laugh so much you're nearly sick! You will wonder how or why you ever existed without these three people.

You find your happy place.

To the younger me, who felt unlovable and was sure she would end up a bearded hermit woman, I want to say this:

1. Don't worry so much.
2. NEVER question your worth.
3. Ask for directions- earlier.
4. Tell more people to fuck off without batting an eyelid.
5. Bleaching your hair doesn't end well.
6. Yes, to tattoos.
7. Listen to your Mama.
8. Study more.
9. Wheat is not your friend.

10. Vodka and cherry-aid is not a fun drink with no consequences.
11. Get more sleep.
12. Learn to protect your soul, it isn't selfish, it's survival.
13. Don't suffer people, they should be in your life if you want them there.
14. Squat more.
15. More sit-ups can't hurt.
16. Comparing yourself to others is optional, choose not to do it.
17. Smile.
18. Swear more.
19. Every day is a blessing.
20. Trust yourself, you know shit.
21. Moisturise - obviously.
22. Don't apologise unless you mother fucking mean it.
23. Keep your cool.
24. Take notes.
25. Eat the kale, your body speaks highly of it.
26. You were never bloody fat!!
27. Save some god damn money.
28. Love more, yes to fun and spontaneity and no to spending your time worrying about the future.
29. Above all, the younger, fuzzy riddled-with-self-doubt version of myself, I want to say this... YOU WIN ALL THE PRIZES!!
30. Love is heading your way- bringing happiness that hits you like a flower-grenade.
31. Finally- and this is important, I can confirm... you will gain control of your hair.

Daddy Issues.

So, I wrote this for me and for anyone else for whom this shoe fits. I speak to a lot of people with Daddy issues. People whose lives are genuinely pierced with a palpable, connected to everything - fault line. They feel the rejection that comes with having an absent father, every day. It renews with every sad song, every event or each time they feel in need of a whiff of patriarchy. I don't want them to feel this way. I want to help them unpretzel their brains.

Let me tell you something that may assist in smashing the void that insists on traipsing around after you. You're not handcuffed to your origins. Everything you do is a choice. If you choose to feel fresh sadness at the thought of rejection, fine. That's your prerogative. Have (no) fun with that. However, you could activate your choices and level up a notch.

Food for thought: -

1.   You were fired out of your dad, probably without thought.
2.   There was likely to have been alcohol involved.
3.   It was a while ago.
4.   There wasn't a lot of forethought or planning.
5.   A future wasn't pictured at that fate-rich time.
6.   Some men can't handle themselves let alone the responsibility of a child.
7.   Some men, don't emotionally develop past the age of twelve.

8. Not everyone is lucky enough or will ever be lucky enough to have you in their lives.

9. OK, you were a seed. But now you are a flower, allow yourself to blossom.

Now, do you still want to attach your self-worth, your esteem and your confidence to something that happened nine months before your first breath?

Here's my advice, I'm big on choices BIG- on choices. Make the choice to value yourself. Choose to protect your feelings. Make a day of it if you need to. A day where you run through all the negative thoughts that could possibly bubble up from absentee Papa Bear. Go sit on the beach, scream into the ocean and throw stones into the waves. Lay on the Earth and forgive yourself for ever doubting your beautiful, fucking worth. You are something else, there's never going to be another one like you. You're motherfucking amazing and the most original, funny and spectacular piece of humanity ever to learn to swear! Now never feel the need to relive this moment.

Tell me again why you padlock your confidence to someone else's pile-of-shit life?

Doesn't make a lot of sense now, does it?

Just know this, some people aren't lucky enough to have YOU as a constant in their lives. That's tough shit for them, not you.

Keep on being a mega human. You have nobody to thank for your life but yourself.

Choose to never doubt your worth again, watch your outlook change.

Dad? Never heard of her...

Old Photos.

I love to sit and study old photos. I run my finger over the glass and take in every tiny detail. I look into the eyes as they, in turn, look back at me and inspect the clothes that were worn. Leaving no inch of the image unturned, I then scan the background for fragments of information about what else was captured in that instant.

Old photos mean so much, especially posthumously. A story of a life lived, a personality, a purpose and of messages, possibly unspoken, yet relayed over time through their quiet, dust-covered omnipresence.

It's funny how these photos take on such a tangible, gilded weight once the person in them has passed. Now, they aren't just pictures. They become a link, a portal for bilateral love. Our way of remembering, communicating, seeking assurances or just relaying pride, even if silently... in thought alone.

I wonder what messages or conversations our loved ones would want us to hear from them if the sepia-toned images became briefly animated. Maybe they'd shout about love, tell us to keep going, or even finish the argument they never got around to winning! One thing I'm sure of though, is they would want us to know how much more than the still, framed image, they really were. Heartbeat and all.

Imagine the life, the love, the struggles and the happiness that a two-dimensional picture doesn't do justice to. How can it?

I have questions...

What made them put on the clothes they were casually immortalised in that day? Why that dress? Why the serious tie? Did they know, when the camera clicked that day, as they sat and manufactured a suitable smile, that next outfit we'd link to them, for eternity would be a mahogany suit?

The value of these time-static images is immeasurable. That's why I love them. The subjects were happy and healthy in that fleeting moment, they really were. Now these images convey emotions and feelings felt in the prime of a life lived, but now done.

Our people, safe and loved - protected by the frame that surrounds them. Taking up their duties now as guardians. Keeping silent look out over their family and friends. They have a front row seat as our lives roll on. The get-togethers, the tears and the laughter. Lots of laughter with induced tears if my home is anything to go by!

Familial pride felt from behind a thin sheet of glass.

So, that's what I get from old photos. It's a lot, isn't it? The messages I perceive are loud and clear because I know what I'll be shouting, when I'm sitting on a shelf. I'll be saying, "I love you", and "I'm so ridiculously proud!"

So, don't put old photos away in a drawer. Put them out on display so they can watch the magic and madness unfold. After all - the past and the present are not mutually exclusive. They fit neatly together to make us who we are.

Low In Fat.

So, Mexico here I come!!

I'm not wondering if I'm 'beach body ready', I'm more concerned if the beach and the bars are ready for me. I've earned every fat cell, muscle and wrinkle. I've been to the gym and pounded the pavements. I've moisturised, waxed and tanned, BUT(T) I'm still not the owner of a sculpted, perfect body!! SO…? I'm alive, I'm healthy and more importantly, HAPPY. Nobody ever died wishing they had more time to finally achieve that last ab. Fuck society and fuck the constant stream of 'perfect' body ideals that shoehorn their way into our psyche! 'Eat this pill, drink this magic tea, waste your cash on a miscellaneous, powdered, chemical shit-storm'. Um, no. How about you fuck off?! My body is comfy to sleep in, bought and paid for AND has grown and nurtured two other humans, I'm PRETTY proud of that! Talking of other humans, I come from (and to) a long line of them, boys and girls, weirdly. I intend to sweat out my confidence so that they get it on them when they're near me, it's my job. I was never a lowercase G. You, you, you and yes, you - we're all GORGEOUS AS FUCK! Deal with it.

Best thing about my body is; it keeps my vital organs safe inside. So, with the hot sand beneath my feet and a bottle of Mexican beer in my hand, I'm going to announce the arrival of my 42-year-old, PERFECTLY IMPERFECT body. I LOVE it!! Well, it is the only one I've got after all!!

DNA My Way.

Deoxyribonucleic acid, I get it. You're strong, you're responsible for encoding my genetic traits. My height, eye colour, my abject stubbornness. Blah, blah, I understand all of this science guff but I want to explain why this is only a fraction of the story.

Yes, I was made, I'm guessing in some teenage exchange of protein, lust and loaded fate. Science suggests then, that I should have turned out very differently. Think of it with the visual aid of this basic metaphor. We start off with a chemical composition, 50% maternal, 50% paternal. Picture a pot of magnolia paint (I thought I'd use it up, there's loads left over in the shed). Yes, that's me, a pot of bland paint, but it's what you put into the tin that gives it its final shade. You might soak up the craziness of the people you grow up with and end up purple. You could add glitter; you might tip in stripes. Stripy paint's a thing isn't it?

What I mean is, yes I turned up on earth, pink, naked and surplus to requirements. But I didn't stay unappreciated for long. My most glorious Mother took me into her brood and tucked me under her wing. I grew up loved and secure in a crazy strong family. My DNA altered. I guess she added glitter and a shitload of unconditional love to my pot of magnolia and the outcome is me!

I wanted to include this in this book, firstly as a shout-out to my Mum who is still going strong, but also to reassure others that we are not caged by our origins. We are who we choose to be. Masters of the universe, err - I mean, of our own destiny. Family isn't always about blood, family are the people that love and protect you, they accept you for who and what you are, and WANT you in their lives.

You may be growing up with Aunts, Uncles, grandparents, even people with no familial link whatsoever. But if there's love there, your fates become entwined. Congratulations, you are now family! Just in case there is any doubt, and this is an attempt to pacify other misplaced kids, think of it like this and then see if DNA is actually that important. I watched a crappy daytime movie once, about two Mothers who had given birth in the same hospital and their babies had been accidentally switched. It was based on a true story, but the acting in this was double pants. Anyway, these women found out years later about the switch, and had to decide what they did about it. Did they swap their eight-year-old kids over, raise a stranger or stick with the child they'd been happily raising? A child they had formed a bond with, nurtured and shared memories and laughter. They decided to stick with the ones they had, leave things as they were, except they set up some sort of visitation program with their genetic children.

I took a lot from this.

I'm not going to lie. Being a cuckoo in a nest of starlings, affects you. I used to wonder why I was different and why couldn't it have happened to someone else, (it does, all the time!) Then I had my own two children. What a life/game changer! I didn't know I was capable of such limitless love. I remembered this shitty film. I sat looking at my two... what if?? What if I discovered in some horrific phone call from the delivery ward, that one of my babies wasn't mine? What if they had been switched? Would I bundle them up, jump in the car and look to exchange for the baby that did share my genes?? Fuck no!! These two human children are mine. I've raised them from what looked like wrinkly, pink rabbits into my extremely funny and unique individuals. They would have to be prized from my decomposing grip.

This helped clear it up once and for all. DNA doesn't matter.

If you didn't share your start with the people you call family, this makes less than NO difference. Family is about helping each other up when we're down. It's sharing a cup of tea when there's only one teabag left. It's a port in a storm, or a cuddle in the scary dark, and love that lasts a lifetime. Although we can't change the beginning of our stories, we can sure as shit have a say in the rest of it.

Birth is vital, death is final, but the bit in between, that bit we call life, that's the bit we share with our family.

Thanks, Mum.

Perfectly Imperfect.

Here's the thing, and yes- this is aimed at you...

You're lazy.

You sleep too much.

You are the crowned queen of procrastination.

You don't always do the right thing.

You promise stuff you know you can't deliver on.

You don't visit folk as much as you should.

Your dedication to finishing that pack of biscuits is beyond reproach.

Your thighs touch and you have miscellaneous hairs growing exactly where they shouldn't.

You could carry a bottle of wine under each boob.

You'd be late to your own funeral.

You don't hit your 5-a-day quota, you haven't since 1995.

It was you.

You love too much and too little.

Your promise to 'get into the gym', is now a national joke. But it's the thought that counts, right?

You are so full of crippling self-doubt that you fear it's visible and may tip out at any moment.

Your underwear doesn't match, EVER.

Your overdraft laughs at you.

You hate to be judged but you judge people anyway.

Your cat has seen some shit and you better hope evolution doesn't fix her voice box.

You develop mohair tights in the winter.

You have breath demons.

Your house is 'tidy'.

You laugh inappropriately at every available wrong moment.

You don't floss every night.

You jiggle when you walk.

You don't know what you want to do but you definitely want to do it.

And...

I know you've drunk booze from a mug.

You're so not like the others...

YOU ARE FUCKING PERFECT!

Cut The Crap.

Here's a question; are you living your best life? Are you living the dream? In the days where social media dominates our realities, we're all so quick to post our polished, filtered images of stuff like holidays, our nights out, fresh manicures, or that amazing lunch that's just arrived in front of us. I do it too, mainly cocktails!

We are however less quick to upload the more mundane, shitty bits of life. How often do you see someone uploading their final demand for payment or their divorce papers? When do you see #fuckmylife trending on Twitter, or a picture of a beautifully filtered, fresh box of anti-depressants? You don't.

One reason people feel pressured to achieve and have it all is the perception that everyone else is gliding through life, with pots of cash, a Prosecco tap in their kitchen and certificate wielding kids that offer to wash up! I'm sorry but I'm going to have to call bullshit!

I say, let's cut the crap. Some days yes, your hair magically goes right. You lose 2lb without trying and it feels like you have a cherub on either side of you gently cupping your boobs and taking the strain off your bra straps. Everything's on a roll. We quickly remember why we developed thumbs and we post this neat reality out into the world so that our friends (list) can see us winning at life.

The thing is we ALL do this. The collective perception is that we are all living, or SHOULD be living, our best life. I want to start 'cut the crap' trending for a change. Let's level the field. Let's bring some

73

fucking honesty into our newsfeeds. I think seeing honest posts will take the pressure off for some of us. Obviously, post the good shit but balance it out with some of the normal shit too. Sometimes you don't pass the test or get the job. Maybe you woke up with a kebab stuck to your face. So? Maybe you're real.

You know that smoking hot selfie, in the amazing new kitchen uploaded by Mrs Perfect Knickers is filtered to the max, right? She doesn't have butterflies round her bonce in real life. Also, she just scooched the crap off her worktop to take that picture, before getting back to emptying the bin.

Life isn't perfect. It isn't supposed to be. It's a work in progress. What you live through makes you who you are! So, let's try to take the good with the bad, the rough with the smooth. Sometimes you're the windscreen others you're the bug. There's a lot to be said for winning, but there's success in failure too. Life is a journey, not a competition, be kind, be real and recognise when we ourselves, or others, need help.

Don't aim for perfection, aim for happiness. The target is bigger.

Force Field.

How are you feeling today? And don't bullshit me or you.   ⌐ow the hell are you, from the centre of your heart- all the way through to your... alarm clock, parking meter, screaming kids and that favour you're doing for what's-her-face? Not too peachy? Maybe you've made an achieve-it-all warrior out of yourself. Maybe you've learnt to claw your way through, deflecting the bad and absorbing the good, with gritted teeth. Gritted teeth and a thin layer of sweat. I'm not going to lie; life can get hard at times.

So, a friend of a friend of a friend of a... you get it. Someone I know, recently and graciously allowed me into her, 'situation.' No names here, no names and no identifying features either. How utterly private and definitely not cause to grab a pen. The reason I'm putting this into type, other than it's easier to read than my mind, is... I encouraged her to start writing down her thoughts. I dangled the invisible carrot of how, simply seeing the thoughts take shape on the page and stretch into paragraphs, can help both the author and reader. Like blue/ black medicine. So, this piece is inspired by her. I gave her the heads up about this, she's happy and is waiting for me to publish it.

She's had a lot to deal with in her young life. A lot, but as I pointed out to her, she had many more beautiful positives than negatives. Her support network is golden. She will triumph over her temporary circumstances and will be fine. But you know what's sitting better with me than fine? I positively know, this shit-ball of blackness she ιs wading through right now, it's making her stronger. She's capable of greatness beyond measure and will soon prove this. She is a mother, so by definition, she is also a fundamentally important role model for her cubs. She knows this too and will be victorious in her search for safety.

Now, as you can tell, what I write is intended to be of some comfort to others, in the form of a handbook on dealing with life. I preach this loudly and often, maybe too often. I preach avidly on confidence, inner strength, empowerment and holding our middle finger aloft. I deliver these snippets of suffragette-isms, in an attempt to sure up and lock and load our collective resilience.

I feel I need to confess that I include myself in my target audience. I get my supply of confidence in mad highs. The top of my inner struttability and power is sometimes so high, the peak is obscured by clouds. I am unbreakable. If you were to cut me, I'd bleed out the rich defiant blood of every female that has ever achieved, defied or surpassed their imposed limitations.

Cool right? Right, only I'm only human. I can and do also get sudden and swift lows. I'll get a hormonal drop-off in my sass levels. This noticeable descent in my strength then goes on to be a self-fulfilling prophecy. Once I've noticed it, I'm wary of it. I can see my inner Beyoncé free-falling into oblivion. I'll hear myself saying the sort of self-deprecating and more worryingly, self-sabotaging comments that I thought I'd locked out of my vocabulary. Pretty sure I nailed that door shut myself! I'll ask my husband if he's sure he loves me. He looks at me like, 'are you fucking high?' Are you reading this shit?

Me, the Queen of being me. The high priestess of 'don't fuck with me,' with a crown adorned with a golden middle finger. Me? How is this crack in my shop front possible?

I'll tell you how, sometimes I'm so fixated on how everyone else is doing, that I don't notice when my own superpower stocks are running low. I sometimes only notice that I'm in need of a glass of mind wine when I've held a one to one support session with someone. I find myself thinking, I needed to hear that!

So, the tool I have in place for when this situation arises, is - I imagine a gorgeous, bulletproof (or insult proof) force field around me. Starting just above my head, going right down to my toes. It envelopes me in a protective layer of reinforcement. The act of placing or imagining this force field around me is what's so powerful. When I feel I need a little help, when the members of Destiny's Child have mentally, briefly left the building, I'll sit. I'll take a moment to remind myself of what a fucking doozy of a confident, capable, insufferably awesome human I am. I'll switch on my protective layer, then I'm ready for all eventualities. It's the equivalent of Dutch courage, without the need for a hip flask.

Now I offer this exercise in self-support to you and the aforementioned friend. You can use it whenever you need, before an interview, exam, family party, or just battling the weekly food shop.

It's free, the force field is for you only. Nobody sees your bubble, so you don't get any odd looks, or no more than is the average amount.

Picture yours how you like, it's your thing. It can be made of iron, glass, a glitter ball, anything. I read somewhere, that one lady made hers of an imaginary perimeter of conkers, because she hated spiders!!

Whatever works I guess.

We can only be strong for so long. When you feel a little in need of a personal protective device, mentally activate that force field. Remind the world who you are and who they think they're fucking with!

Question Everything.

If I told you that the common denominator in all my interactions with folk, and I mean ALL- has been my itchy questionitus you'd understand why I'm a metaphorical table flipper.

Growing up I'd always wondered why? Why I should be quiet, why it was so important to eat broccoli, why I needed to go to bed when it was still light out, and why adults got to drink beer and I didn't... Perplexing, huh?

Then as I got older, I got a whole new load of provoked question opportunities. Namely, why did I have to toe the line, hand in my homework, put that fag out, and why was sitting up straight the bloody be all and end all?! Why? Because somebody else other than me, required it to happen. To enable THEIR day to go a little smoother. So that the collective wine consumption of the school staff wouldn't take such a nightly hit?

I still question everything now. It's my theme. Other people collect handbags, I question stuff. Lately, I've been questioning why we feel obliged to keep people in our lives, when they repeatedly, hurt, ignore or step over you to get to someone else. Why? Because we're supposed to? Who says? My instincts are finely tuned, you could cut glass with them. Mine tell me to avoid those around me that make me feel like shit, or that I'm second best. To those, I offer a framed print of my middle finger.

As I hand this Banksy inspired piece of mind art over, I feel instantly lighter, happier. Why should we allow someone else's low love levels to seep into our self-esteem? I guess it's the old blood is thicker than water thing, and yes it is. But you know what's thicker still? Peace of mind. I'm no longer offering my heart as a place for anyone to wipe their feet.

Questioning stuff has its purpose. For me, it has spurred me on, I asked why I couldn't achieve what I wanted to, just because I was told I couldn't. Now I question EVERYTHING, from what's in my food, to what better deals I can get on stuff. Why I shouldn't sleep in till 10.00 and why I should feel bad about it. I don't, by the way.

Being such an ask-hole has helped me out on many occasions. Like asking the pharmacist why I'd been given the wrong pills? Could have ended badly! Or the time I went for a specialist appointment at the hospital, about the muscles in my hands. They're a bit temperamental. He asked me to take off my shoes, socks and jeans just to rule things out. What the fuck? I thought about it for a millisecond. Did I want to do that? No, I bloody didn't. I politely told him, I wasn't going to do that at any point, now or in the future. He just looked warm and said, "Err ...OK".

Up yours, if I don't like it, I'm not doing it.

What inspired this writing sesh, was an incident I witnessed in the supermarket the other day. So, I'm queuing up to pay for my 'vegetables,' and stuff. There were about three people in front of me. I was happy to wait. There was also one woman waiting behind me.

She was looking around thinking the same thing as me. 'Why, have fifteen checkouts and only four open?' Good question love.

Then, a staff member walks over to her and suggests that she move to a till she was about to open. The lady behind had already clocked four other people, beer, loo rolls and crisps clutched to their chests, setting up the same goal, the free checkout! She says to the store worker, "no thanks, I'll stop here". Again, the staff lady suggested she move. Three times she asked, tapping her finger on the conveyor belt all the time. I was waiting to see the ending now. The woman behind me folds her arms and shouts, "are you asking me or bloody telling me, love?!" LOUDLY. I wasn't expecting that. She knew what she wanted and wasn't wearing her sheep coat that day. She questioned her situation and stood her ground, a little aggressively but the thought was there. I smiled at her, "nice work", I said.

OK so it was a mini moment, but I couldn't help wondering who of us would have just shuffled into position, by-passing our own thoughts. Fallen in line without asking why?

I want you to think about what you're doing and why? Does the situation continue to serve you? Does it make you happy? Did it ever? Do you want to do it? Are you OK?

If the answer is no, it's time to get a new plan.

Question everything, just to rule out the possibility that it's not a goer. Maybe it is, but at least you'll know and have peace of mind moving forward.

You'll know it's right, right?

You'll know because you've checked.

Bloom Where You're Planted.

To be sat in the epicentre of your life, right there- slap bang, right where you should be, that is the ultimate in fortune. How lucky are we to live in such a mesmerizingly beautiful spot on the planet? After all, where we find ourselves blooming is really a matter of luck. Luck and basic geography.

I used to lie awake wondering what else was out there. When you're fourteen and as rebellious and disaffected as a one-girl military coup, you get bored with your surroundings. The globe seemed small enough to hop around on. Stick a pin in a map, that kind of thing. I'm glad I chose to stay. I've raised my children in the clean salty air this coastline is famous for.

The map of my hometown is like my seat. A comfy chair complete with arse-groove. It's full of familiar faces and buildings that spew memories from their seams. This town is a shored-up, stabilisers on, cupboard full, beauty of a place. Tell me, why would I need to roam off?

There's a lot to be said then, for blooming where you're planted. To feel genuine contentedness and pride in being able to claim Weymouth as my home. To set down roots and watch the flowers of my life, blossom, this is where happiness lies. Happiness is good for your mental and heart health.

My advice, if you're having a shitty day; go outside, take your shoes off. Look out to the horizon, the view is literally golden! You've paid for your cup by living here, now step outside for all-day-long, get-it-whilst-it's-hot, free refills! Refills of pure, sea infected, lungsful.

Flowers do best when they bloom where they're planted. People do that too.

If You Tolerate This…

What are you going to tolerate today?

Here's an extendable list of shit I want you to be prepared for. Prepared so that you can adjust your acceptance levels and not suffer in silence. What you put up with on a daily basis becomes the blueprint for your children's lives. So be mindful, only pass on good habits.

**clears throat.

- Rudeness
- Bad service
- Emotional blackmail
- Being short-changed
- Cheating
- Violence
- Being put-upon
- Assumptions
- Shitty comments
- Shady looks
- Bitching
- The shittiest government since 1945
- Parking charges
- Donald Trump
- Political correctness
- Global desolation
- War

- Animal cruelty
- Reality stars
- Racism
- Homophobia
- Jealousy
- Letting people walk over you
- Self-deprecation
- Bad parenting
- Dishonesty
- Poor excuses
- Bad jobs
- People pleasing
- Wastefulness
- Eminem's Mum
- Bad wine
- Tampon tax
- Limitations
- The fucking Kardashian's
- Ageism
- Attempting to privatise the NHS
- Single use plastics
- Cold callers
- Sexual harassment
- Celery
- Bad music
- Brexit bollocks
- Unkindness

The list goes on...

OK, so I might be going through my Manic Street Preachers phase again but it's true!

What we tolerate our kids will automatically assume is OK. What we accept as normal becomes the hand we deal to the next generation. That would be fine, only the next batch of humans are my... your... OUR kids!

Don't tolerate for a second something that you wouldn't want your kids to have to deal with.

Lead from the very front of the front. Practice your swear words (in the mirror) acquire a soapbox, use it.

Make your children, your grandchildren and their kids proud. Not forgetting your ancestors.

What's stopping you?

Get going… and wait for me!!

Home Guard Hero.

Grandad, I think I can see things through your eyes, I really do. I know we never met but you know me, and I feel I know a bit about you. I feel your family pride and your hand-me-down strength, (I think we all got that). I've heard Mum talk about your skills as the town butcher, and because this was a 'reserved occupation,' you volunteered for the local defence instead of going off to war. It's these stories that really come alive, the ones of you being a great Home guardsman. What an honour as well as a huge responsibility you must have felt. Your brothers also joined you in looking after Wincanton and of course, its people.

You would deliver supplies of food to the townspeople by day and put them before yourself at night. Going around the buildings, making sure everyone was safely locked up, and had all they needed. Looking out for anything suspicious. Did you feel like a hero? I'm sure that you didn't. You would have just got on with the job in hand, doing your wartime duty, modest about your exploits.

I've walked down Mill Street, Grandad and been inside your old house. It's beautiful, but what I gained most out of the experience was how real you were. How real your need to protect your children was, as well as the rest of the town. What better, hands-on and practical way of defending your patch against the imminence of invasion by the enemy, than by patrolling the Somerset countryside? You know... if you say that quickly it's unremarkable. But, Grandad, I am able to experience some of the enormity of your endeavours.

I've read so much and asked so many questions, that some of your history has become mine. What a gift, what a legacy!

It is through your protection and selflessness that you are now the proud owner of three or four football teams worth of children, grandchildren and great-grandchildren, and yes, they keep on coming. New faces joining the team, all able to keep your lineage going. Another reason for your distant pride.

Over the summer I'm planning on taking Mum on a road trip. We'll walk around your old town and have lunch in the Red Lion, she recalls how you would take her in there with you, lifting her on to the bar so she could sing her little heart out for the regulars. She beamed when she told me this, of course you know... I think you were there as she took a stroll down memory lane. We'll also try to locate the place where your rifle accidentally went off during cleaning. Nobody was hurt thankfully, or this story may have had an alternative ending! I didn't want your accomplishments to be forgotten, covered in dust in the vaults of history, so this is going in my book, I hope you like it.

What I wouldn't bloody give for half an hour in a beer garden with you...

Churchill named you (collectively) as The Home Guard.

I know you better, as Charles Frederick Lionel Chatfield (1900-1972), My Grandad.

A Person-Shaped Hole.

Yesterday I attended the funeral of an old school friend. She wasn't by any means a close friend; I hadn't spoken to her in years. She was more of a friend of friends. I went to show solidarity to her family, my friends and out of respect. Respect that one of our year from school had lost her life.

I wasn't going to go, I kept alternating between, 'yes, OK-I'll go,' to 'no, definitely not, I'm not doing it.' In the end, I felt compelled to just be in the crowd. To recognise the fact that a young woman, a wife, mother, sister and daughter had lost her battle to survive.

As I stood at the back of a tightly packed sea of black, my autism flavoured emotions ran amok. I became aware that my face was wet. I'm standing there in silence with ten million thoughts running through my brain. Life is ridiculously precious. That could have been any of us up the front there. Having their best moments held up for all to see. I knew then that my salty cheeks represented so much more than the loss of a fellow class of '92 member. These thoughts almost knocked me off my feet. I'm a fainter, I also absorb other people's emotions. Here I was, stood up to my neck in the sadness of a packed room of mourners. Fight or flight? I feel hot and cold and wonder if I might pass out. Please no! So, I gather my thoughts and focus on my breathing. Soon it is over, and we step out into the cold March air.

Now I am thoughtful, thoughtful and ridiculously teary. I knew this would happen. Funerals and I mean ALL funerals, even of people I didn't know, literally pull the rug from under my feet. My worry mode is activated, and it doesn't turn off in a hurry. I attempt to literally drown my worries in booze. I get to thinking how, in the blink of an eye we can become a memory. A prominently placed photo in a special frame, or the reason your family seek out psychics or mediums. I don't want to be a memory. I want to be real. I want to live to meet my children's children. I want to experience being confused by the younger generation and to not know when I'm about to fart! I want to have the luxury of grey hair and creaking bones. I want to go when the time is right.

My writing, as always is influenced by my daily adventures of being a fuzzball. This experience like many before has reinforced my opinion that we should love and respect our lives. We should look after our bodies and cherish our health. We don't know what tomorrow brings. Tell your people you love them, forgive the meaningless disagreements, feel everything. Everything!

Life is short, shorter for some than others. While death has no chance of breaking the bonds of love, it can leave behind a person-shaped hole. I don't know much, but I am sure that those that get taken too early, go on ahead to get things ready for the rest of us. We all meet up again eventually and the cycle of love, life and laughter continues.

Hug the shit out of your family and be thankful that your heart still beats.

Where Can I Stick This Broom?

I saw a quote the other day, it said 'I may not be Wonder Woman, but I can do things that'll make you wonder...' I snorted like a pig to this whilst raising my eyebrows so high, I almost gave myself a fringe. Sometimes I wonder how I manage to get in all of the stuff that finds itself scribbled onto my job list. Yes, I have a job list, don't you? I think it's because, these days we're expected to be all things to everyone.

What I mean by that is, society requires us to tick so many boxes. Be a good wife/girlfriend/ Mum/human. Find the time to make yourself look half decent. No pressure but have you seen the photoshopped standard of a 'naturally' beautiful woman these days? Complete with the toned, tanned baboon butt, hair-free, tits till next Tuesday thing they all seem to have going on?

I just manage an irregular, monthly eyebrow appointment, and not for anything fancy. I'm happy with a tidy up. Somewhere in my bathroom routine, I'll grapple with a razor and a self-tan mitt. Sometimes at the same time. That's after a gym and Slendertone sesh! Oh, please don't think I spend any serious time on this faff. These attempts at home body editing, are squeezed in around the rest of the rapacious demands that befall a regular, busy woman-o-gram.

I feel like these days there are too many normalised demands placed on us, just simply to maintain a certain level of presentability. We must look after ourselves, our partners and kids. We should (ideally) keep them fed, watered and clothed AND where possible, problem free. Have they done their homework, kept their appointments, charged their phones, taken a shit? Please wash your hands! Amongst all of this, we should find the time, between sunrise and sunset to do the housework, re-stock the fridge, do the laundry (fuck the ironing, that's an ask too far!) and walk the dog, all whilst trying to not look like a maniac.

There's a big pressure to have everything taken care of. To have your to-do list completed, and find time for coherent conversation on current affairs, without, I might add, the need to bite anyone. Bit farfetched if you ask me.

Now, I'm all for bucking the trend of societal demands but it appears we are doomed if we fall in line and extra doomed if we don't. If we Stepford ourselves into the agreeable, loving, still looks OK for her age, ooh are these homemade? Thanks for the sarnies type of female, then - we are 'doing too much.' We should 'try to relax, take some timeout.'

BELLY LAUGH!

It's a different story when you get unannounced visitors after a hardcore cocktail session. Your washing up is winking at you and you've run out of milk/loo rolls/energy and fucks to give. You have managed, in a single evening to lose all your brownie points, you are now a cause for concern and possible functioning/closet alcoholic. Well, like spinach in my teeth I have a little 'fuck you,' in my smile...

As I write this, I have just done three loads of washing and hung it all out to dry in the sun. I've cleaned both bathrooms and made three beds. I've done 'some' ironing, whilst using up every swear word known to mankind. I've walked the dog and hoovered the stairs. All this when all I wanted to do today was write and sample coffees from around the world. I'm still waiting for my writing shed, it's on my husband's to-do list. He hasn't ticked it off or started it yet!

I've come to realise that half of the pressures we feel or believe we must bow to come from ourselves. Nobody other than me will notice that the bin lid has been wiped or that my nails are shinier than yesterday, because nobody noticed them then either. How about we relax and do stuff just to please ourselves. Let's stop with the expectations we think we are under.

Some days it's OK to do the bare minimum. As long as your teeth are clean and you've flushed the loo, you're still a functioner, right? Sometimes it's fine to feel the sofa begin to slowly absorb your arse cheeks. It's all about balance.

Life is short and no one ever stood at a graveside and remembered the dead by their enviably completed ironing pile. So, fuck the regime even if it is 50% of our own making. Do what feels right for you and only that. I know I will, just stick a broom up my arse, at least I can get the floors done as I quietly rebel.

Your Name Here.

I hope you have a big fat marker pen somewhere nearby; you'll need it after you've read this. This offering circles over the head of the topic of willpower. Dropping shit-bombs on any self-doubt or tired out patterns of behaviour.

So, willpower - they say you either have it by the bucket load, or you don't. Some of us can resist the cake, beer, crack- pipe... more than others. These lucky people have more chance of beating their demons, or throat punching their negative thoughts into oblivion, am I right?

No, my bullshit detector is currently showing some pretty high readings. I am once again calling out the tired, battered old belief systems that we use to prop ourselves up. There is no fabled, lucky individual who seems blessed with superhuman internal strength. I'm 99.9% sure that the people that say 'I can't do it' or 'I just don't have the willpower' are ultimately giving themselves a back out clause. Mentally writing themselves a permission slip for future fuckups.

The truth is we all have willpower in limitless and self-renewing supply! Once you've resisted one fag, or whatever is your gig, you're energised, better equipped for the next temptation. It's like a plant, it grows in size and strength. It just needs the right conditions. Water it, the blossoms are beautiful. Switch on this evergreen new strength and watch the life prizes roll in.

I've been told in the past that I've got mad willpower skills. Seemingly, when I make my mind up to do something it's done. Simple, no ifs, no I'm not ready or buts. Here's my take on it though. I don't have a steel rod shoved up my arse, reinforcing my good choice levels. I just take a minute and mentally weigh up the 'what if I do and what if I don't' future feelings.

The same mental arithmetic happens in other situations where my apparently bionic strength is called for. It's not hard, I'm not different. When people say, 'I'm sorry, I tried to stop smoking/ drinking/ being a turd, (other vices are available) but I couldn't. It was too hard'. My first thought is - really?! I interpret 'it was too hard' as, I felt some discomfort, my old well-worn, trusty past behaviours have served me... OK-ish, so I'll carry on. *Yawn*.

Wrongo.

Give this little exercise a try. If you weren't blessed with hot and cold running will. Wallpaper your heart with images of your loved ones, your family, your team. Have them as a constant reminder of who you'd be letting down, if you choose the easy way out.

You can carry on.

You can be better.

You can be the best version of you.

Don't let choosing the easy option, or fear of change stand in the way of happiness.

So, who has a new supply of willpower?

↑↑↑↑↑↑↑↑ YOUR NAME HERE ↑↑↑↑↑↑↑↑

BV - #0011 - 210420 - C0 - 210/148/6 - PB - 9781912243877